Little People, **BIG DREAMS**

DAVID ATTENBOROUGH

Written by
Maria Isabel Sánchez Vegara

Illustrated by
Mikyo Noh

Frances Lincoln
Children's Books

Little David grew up in Leicester, England, with his parents and two brothers. His father was the head of the local university, and they lived on campus: a great place for curious minds.

David loved nature and animals. Ants, birds, chameleons…he was fascinated by all the species he read about in books and wished he could meet them in real life.

He often went for long bike rides to find and collect fossils. There was something amazing about plants and animals that were thousands of years old.

One day, David received a package from
a friend with a new piece for his collection—
a dried seahorse! It wasn't his birthday, but
it was the day he decided to become a naturalist.

David studied geology and zoology and obtained a degree in natural science. But he didn't want to just observe animals—he wanted to meet them, too.

David started to work as a broadcaster in television, a new technology at the time. He brought animals from the zoo to the studio. They were very entertaining guests!

But David wanted to film the animals in their natural habitats—their homes. He started to go on trips all over the world. Wherever he went, he made new friends.

He met turtles on the Galapagos Islands and gorillas in the African jungle. When he visited Antarctica, he was introduced to all the members of a penguin family.

One of his shows, *Wildlife on One*, became
the most popular in British history. It was a great program
about biology that united audiences of all generations.

Later, David was honored for his incredible documentaries about life on our planet. He also received a knighthood and is today called Sir David.

Electrotettix
Attenboroughi

Cascolus Ravitis

Euptychia
Attenborough

RRS SIR DAVID ATTENBOROUGH

Materpiscis
Attenboroughi

Microleo
Attenboroughi

Prethopalpus
Attenboroughi

Nepenthes
Attenboroughii

Many animals and plants were named after him:
a rare butterfly, a snail, a prehistoric lion, a spider...
even a carnivorous plant!

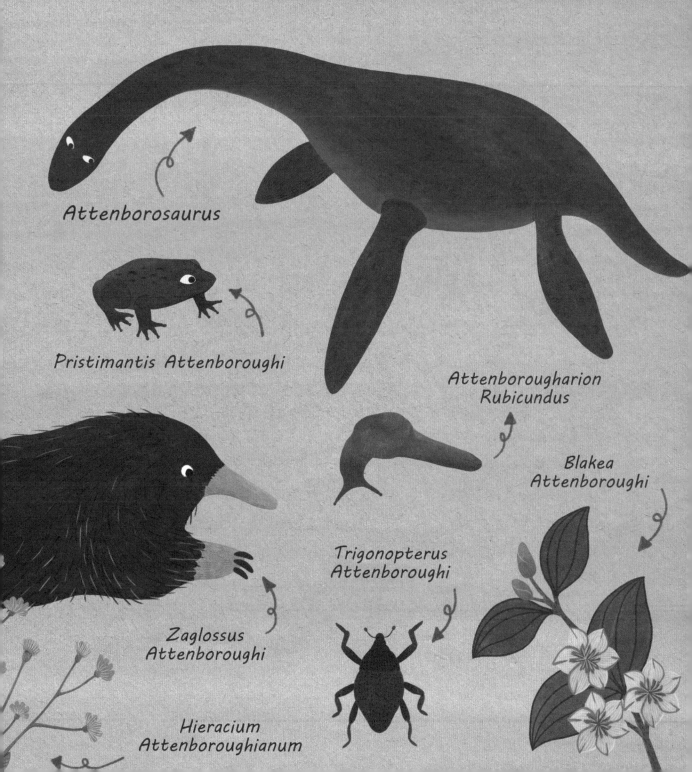

Attenborosaurus

Pristimantis Attenboroughi

Attenborougharion
Rubicundus

Blakea
Attenboroughi

Trigonopterus
Attenboroughi

Zaglossus
Attenboroughi

Hieracium
Attenboroughianum

Today, David continues to care about the natural world. Wherever he goes, he encourages people to do their best to look after it, and believes that humans have the power to preserve it.

And little David still looks at the world as if it's huge and unexplored. Because there are always new things to discover if you take the time to look for them.

DAVID ATTENBOROUGH

(Born 1926)

c. 1936

1955

David Attenborough was born into an educated family in Leicester, England. His mother was a linguist and his father, a professor. As a child, fossil hunting and collecting nature specimens became David's passion. This appetite for learning stayed with him, and as a young man, David won a scholarship to study zoology and geology at Cambridge University. His studies were paused when he was called up for national service in the Royal Navy in 1947, but he later returned to gain another degree in anthropology. Combining a love for the natural world with an understanding of human behavior, David become known for his unique approach to broadcasting at the BBC. Speaking in a hushed tone full of excitement, David filmed

1956   2015

his first shows in 1957: *The Pattern of Animals* and *Zoo Quest*.
He wanted to find ways to connect audiences to the natural world,
and the opportunity to do so came about when color television was
introduced to the BBC in 1967. His groundbreaking series *Life on
Earth* transported audiences from their living rooms to the wild in a
totally new way. This was the first of many pioneering shows, including
Wildlife on One, *The Private Life of Plants*, and *Blue Planet*, all of
which changed human understanding about our place in nature.
David believed that "no one will protect what they don't care about;
and no one will care about what they have never experienced." In his
nineties, David continues to make audiences all over the world care.

Want to find out more about **David Attenborough?**
Read one of these great books:

Super Scientists: David Attenborough by Sarah Ridley
David Attenborough: Naturalist Visionary by Sonya Newland

BOARD BOOKS

COCO CHANEL	MAYA ANGELOU	FRIDA KAHLO	AMELIA EARHART	MARIE CURIE	ADA LOVELACE	ROSA PARKS

ISBN: 978-1-78603-245-4   ISBN: 978-1-78603-249-2   ISBN: 978-1-78603-247-8   ISBN: 978-1-78603-252-2   ISBN: 978-1-78603-253-9   ISBN:978-1-78603-259-1   ISBN:978-1-78603-263-8

EMMELINE PANKHURST   AUDREY HEPBURN   ELLA FITZGERALD

ISBN: 978-1-78603-261-4   ISBN: 978-1-78603-255-3   ISBN:978-1-78603-257-7

BOX SETS

WOMEN IN ART   WOMEN IN SCIENCE

ISBN: 978-1-78603-428-1   ISBN: 978-1-78603-429-8

BOOKS & PAPER DOLLS

EMMELINE PANKHURST   MARIE CURIE
ISBN: 978-1-78603-400-7   ISBN: 978-1-78603-401-4

Collect the
Little People, **BIG DREAMS** series:

FRIDA KAHLO   COCO CHANEL   MAYA ANGELOU

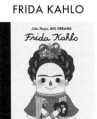  

ISBN: 978-1-84780-783-0   ISBN: 978-1-84780-784-7   ISBN: 978-1-84780-889-9

AMELIA EARHART

ISBN: 978-1-84780-888-2

AGATHA CHRISTIE

ISBN: 978-1-84780-960-5

MARIE CURIE

ISBN: 978-1-84780-962-9

ROSA PARKS

ISBN: 978-1-78603-018-4

AUDREY HEPBURN

ISBN: 978-1-78603-053-5

EMMELINE PANKHURST

ISBN: 978-1-78603-020-7

ELLA FITZGERALD

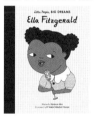

ISBN: 978-1-78603-087-0

ADA LOVELACE

ISBN: 978-1-78603-076-4

JANE AUSTEN

ISBN: 978-1-78603-120-4

GEORGIA O'KEEFFE

ISBN: 978-1-78603-122-8

HARRIET TUBMAN

ISBN: 978-1-78603-227-0

ANNE FRANK

ISBN: 978-1-78603-229-4

MOTHER TERESA

ISBN: 978-1-78603-230-0

JOSEPHINE BAKER

ISBN: 978-1-78603-228-7

L. M. MONTGOMERY

ISBN: 978-1-78603-233-1

JANE GOODALL

ISBN: 978-1-78603-231-7

SIMONE DE BEAUVOIR

ISBN: 978-1-78603-232-4

MUHAMMAD ALI

ISBN: 978-1-78603-331-4

STEPHEN HAWKING

ISBN: 978-1-78603-333-8

MARIA MONTESSORI

ISBN: 978-1-78603-755-8

VIVIENNE WESTWOOD

ISBN: 978-1-78603-757-2

MAHATMA GANDHI

ISBN: 978-1-78603-787-9

DAVID BOWIE

ISBN: 978-1-78603-332-1

WILMA RUDOLPH

ISBN: 978-1-78603-751-0

DOLLY PARTON

ISBN: 978-1-78603-760-2

BRUCE LEE

ISBN: 978-0-7112-4629-4

RUDOLF NUREYEV

ISBN: 978-1-78603-791-6

ZAHA HADID

ISBN: 978-0-7112-4641-6

MARY SHELLEY

ISBN: 978-0-7112-4639-3

MARTIN LUTHER KING JR.

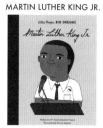

ISBN: 978-0-7112-4567-9

Brimming with creative inspiration, how-to projects, and useful information to enrich your everyday life, Quarto Knows is a favorite destination for those pursuing their interests and passions. Visit our site and dig deeper with our books into your area of interest: Quarto Creates, Quarto Cooks, Quarto Homes, Quarto Lives, Quarto Drives, Quarto Explores, Quarto Gifts, or Quarto Kids.

Text © 2020 Maria Isabel Sánchez Vegara. Illustrations © 2020 Mikyo Noh.

First Published in the US in 2020 by Frances Lincoln Children's Books, an imprint of The Quarto Group.

400 First Avenue North, Suite 400, Minneapolis, MN 55401, USA.

T (612) 344-8100 F (612) 344-8692 www.QuartoKnows.com

First Published in Spain in 2020 under the title Pequeño & Grande David Attenborough

by Alba Editorial, s.l.u., Baixada de Sant Miquel, 1, 08002 Barcelona

www.albaeditorial.es

ISBN 978-0-7112-4564-8

Set in Futura BT.

Published by Katie Cotton • Designed by Karissa Santos

Edited by Rachel Williams and Katy Flint • Production by Nicolas Zeifman

Manufactured in Guangdong, China CC112019

9 7 5 3 1 2 4 6 8

Photographic acknowledgments (pages 28–29, from left to right) 1. David Attenborough school photograph, c. 1936 © Leicester Mercury Picture 2. David Attenborough with his son, Robert, and coatimundi © 1955 PA/PA Archive/PA Images 3. A portrait of British naturalist and broadcaster David Attenborough, 1956 © Popperfoto via Getty Images 4. David Attenborough, 2015 © Neale Haynes via Getty Images

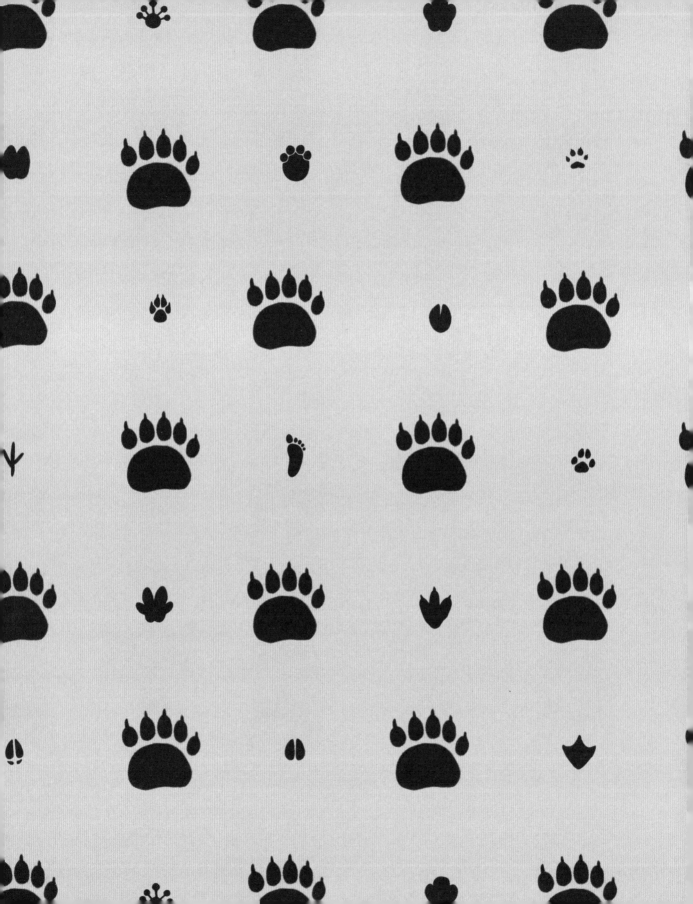